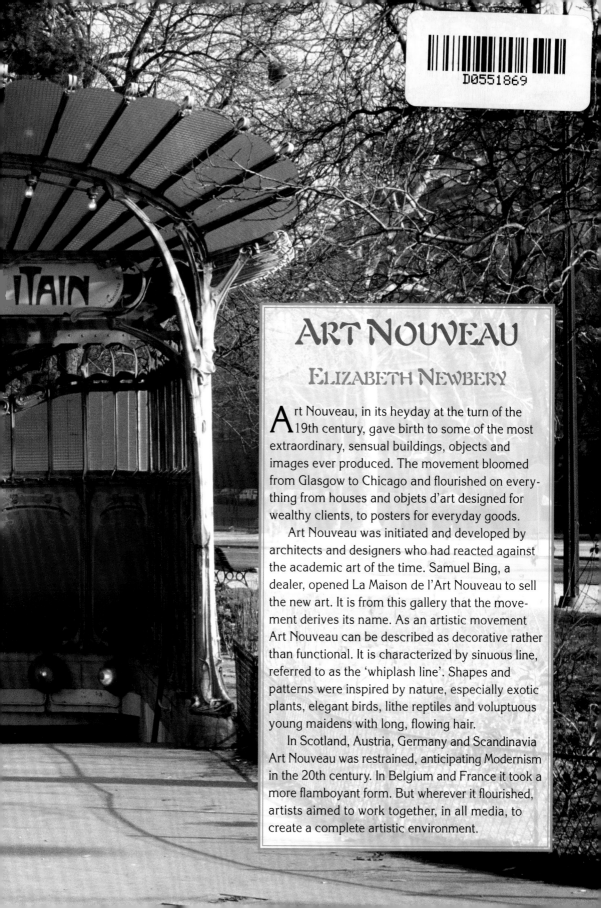

Art Nouveau

Elizabeth Newbery

Art Nouveau, in its heyday at the turn of the 19th century, gave birth to some of the most extraordinary, sensual buildings, objects and images ever produced. The movement bloomed from Glasgow to Chicago and flourished on everything from houses and objets d'art designed for wealthy clients, to posters for everyday goods.

Art Nouveau was initiated and developed by architects and designers who had reacted against the academic art of the time. Samuel Bing, a dealer, opened La Maison de l'Art Nouveau to sell the new art. It is from this gallery that the movement derives its name. As an artistic movement Art Nouveau can be described as decorative rather than functional. It is characterized by sinuous line, referred to as the 'whiplash line'. Shapes and patterns were inspired by nature, especially exotic plants, elegant birds, lithe reptiles and voluptuous young maidens with long, flowing hair.

In Scotland, Austria, Germany and Scandinavia Art Nouveau was restrained, anticipating Modernism in the 20th century. In Belgium and France it took a more flamboyant form. But wherever it flourished, artists aimed to work together, in all media, to create a complete artistic environment.

THE GROWTH of ART NOUVEAU

Art Nouveau had its roots in England, and grew from the Arts and Crafts movement founded in 1861 by William Morris. An influential artist, he rejected the mass-produced goods that cluttered mid-Victorian homes and called for the return of the skilled artisan of the Middle Ages.

Artists in England took up Morris' aim to revitalize design. They looked towards a myriad of sources as diverse as interlacing Celtic patterns, the curves of Gothic architecture, Pre-Raphaelite painting and symbolism, the fresh, linear illustrations of Walter Crane, the mystical work of William Blake and, especially, all aspects of Japanese art.

Art Nouveau began to take shape as a movement in the 1880s. It was popularized through London shops such as Liberty & Co and Ambrose Heal, who both sold designs by Art Nouveau artists. The annual exhibitions of the Arts and Crafts Exhibition Society, beginning in 1888, and publications such as *The Studio*, a magazine first published in 1893, disseminated the style rapidly and spread the movement to Europe and, to a lesser extent, the USA.

Art Nouveau first appeared on the Continent in Belgium in the work of the architect Victor Horta. In France, the style flourished in the designs of the architect Hector Guimard, the glassmaker Émile Gallé, the furniture designer Louis Majorelle, the jeweller René Lalique and in the posters of Alphonse Mucha. In Germany, as the Jugendstil, and in Vienna, as the Sezessionstil, it reached a peak in the furniture of

Josef Hoffmann and the exotic paintings of Gustav Klimt. In Scotland, Charles Rennie Mackintosh spearheaded a sober version known as the Glasgow School. In Spain, Antonio Gaudí designed highly individual buildings that give the impression of natural, growing forms. In the USA, the leading figure was Louis Comfort Tiffany, whose iridescent glass vases and stained-glass lampshades were exported extensively to Europe in the 1890s.

ABOVE: Blake wrote and illustrated poems that he published in books made by himself. This illustration for the title page of The Songs of Innocence, *published in 1789, anticipates Art Nouveau illustration with its emphasis on the close integration of linear illustration and hand-drawn lettering.*

BELOW: This chair was designed about 1882 by Arthur Mackmurdo, an English architect, graphic artist and craftsman. It is usually considered to be the earliest example of Art Nouveau.

ABOVE: Archer and seated fisherman observe a ship across waves by Yoshitoshi,1879. Japanese prints with their flattened perspectives, sparing use of colour and line, and subject matter placed asymmetrically and drawn from nature, were a major source of inspiration.

ARCHITECTURE & INTERIOR DESIGN

Artists and architects attracted to Art Nouveau were interested in modernity and urbanity. Architects concentrated on building in the great cities of Europe such as Glasgow, Paris, Brussels, Amsterdam, Prague, Vienna and Barcelona. In the USA they built in New York, St Louis and Chicago. Those cities still have Art Nouveau buildings but most of the architects are now long forgotten.

Architects were united in their aim to design exteriors and interiors to produce a harmonious whole. Modern materials of the time, such as cast iron used with glass, allowed light, airy structures and new decorative possibilities. Exteriors had smooth, rounded corners, asymmetrical façades and decorative ironwork based on twisting plant forms. Inside, room settings had co-ordinated colour schemes with carefully thought through details such as door hinges and specially designed furniture.

The Belgian architect Victor Horta was the first to design buildings in the Art Nouveau style. Most of his commissions were unique, demanding huge economic resources from his wealthy clientele. His first major work, the Tassel House in Brussels, erected in 1893, is considered to be the most complete expression of Continental Art Nouveau combining two-dimensional and three-dimensional design. Many of the interiors were decorated with English wallpapers and silks from Liberty & Co.

In Paris, Hector Guimard was the leading exponent of Art Nouveau, adapting Horta's style to great effect. Guimard is best known for the entrances he designed to the Paris Metro (illustrated on inside front cover). Elsewhere in Paris many of the most extravagant Art Nouveau buildings were shops,

LEFT: The stairwell in the house that Horta designed for himself in 1898–1901, now the Horta House Museum, Brussels.

INSET: Detail of the stair railing in Horta's house.

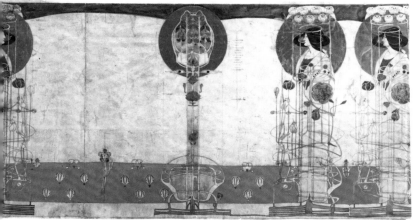

LEFT: Mackintosh's designs for stencilled murals (1896) for Miss Cranston's tearooms, Buchanan Street, Glasgow. The ghostly figures of women caused critics to call Mackintosh and his contemporaries 'The Spook School'.

5

cafés and restaurants designed by obscure architects working on low budgets.

In Scotland, Charles Rennie Mackintosh working mainly in Glasgow produced elegant, austere architecture, never allowing an excess of decoration. He designed several houses near Glasgow, but his fame rests primarily on the designs for the Glasgow School of Art and those for four tearooms in Glasgow.

In Barcelona, Antonio Gaudí made his most original contributions to the Art Nouveau movement as it began to decline in the rest of Europe. His work attracted the attention of Eusebio de Guell, a wealthy industrialist, for whom he carried out many important commissions. These included Park Guell (1900–14), a fantasy of columns disguised as stone trees, reptilian fountains and decorated throughout with broken pieces of colourful pottery set in concrete.

RIGHT: In 1883, Gaudí designed his spectacular masterpiece, the Church of the Sagrada Família, unfinished at his death in 1926.

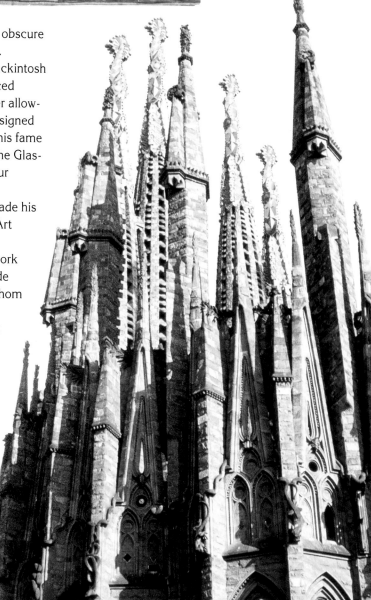

FURNITURE

Furniture was made to complement particular architectural settings and was the work of architects, rather than cabinet-makers. It displayed similar characteristics to the buildings and interiors for which it was designed, having rounded contours and sinuous lines. It was often decorated with plants, insects and the curvaceous bodies of women.

Early furniture designers were the Belgian architects Victor Horta and Henri van de Velde. Like his buildings, Horta's furniture was unique for each client and none was made to be reproduced commercially. Van de Velde, originally an Impressionist painter, based his furniture on aesthetic theories set down by the French Impressionists Seurat and Signac.

LEFT: High-backed oak chair painted white, decorated with a rose stencil. Made by Mackintosh in 1902.

ABOVE: Bed with decoration based on plant forms by Majorelle, circa 1900.

In France, the architect Hector Guimard designed asymmetrical, heavily carved freeform furniture and the glassmaker Émile Gallé also designed some of the most opulent Art Nouveau furniture decorated with plant and flower motifs. Louis Majorelle, perhaps the greatest designer of Art Nouveau furniture, produced luxurious pieces also inspired by nature.

In Scotland, Charles Rennie Mackintosh produced more austere furniture in stained or painted oak, relieved with elegant inlays of metal or stained glass. His first major commission for Miss Cranston's tearooms in Glasgow included all the furniture and fittings, chairs, card tables, umbrella stands and cutlery.

In Germany and Austria the designers were the first to face up to the reality of mass production. Seeing that machines were unable to reproduce elaborate decoration, they searched for an alternative solution where function was as important as aesthetics. Josef Hoffmann pioneered the search and his later designs for bentwood furniture manufactured from 1903 by Kohn and Thonet have become classics of early 20th-century design.

ABOVE: An étagère (a stand with open shelves for displaying ornaments) by Gallé, circa 1900.

7

ABOVE: Koloman Moser, an Austrian, was a close associate of Hoffmann. In his later work, like this cupboard made in 1904, he used geometric shapes as decorative motifs. The female figures inlaid with metal and mother-of-pearl, show the influence of Mackintosh (see page 5).

POSTERS & ILLUSTRATION

The emphasis of Art Nouveau on two-dimensional linear design meant that some of the greatest contributions to the movement were made in the field of graphic art – particularly posters and book illustration. Imagine the effect in Paris at the turn of the century when Guimard's exuberant designs decorated Metro entrances, and hoardings were adorned with some of the most stunning posters ever produced.

ABOVE: An illustration for La Dame aux Camelias *by Beardsley.*

Left and Opposite Far Left: Mucha was responsible for creating the definitive pin-up girl of Art Nouveau. He used her on whatever he was designing, whether it was textiles, stained glass, sculpture or jewellery.

Below: A page from Flora's Feast, *a children's book written and illustrated by Crane and published by Cassell and Company, 1895.*

9

France was the centre of poster design largely because of the interest the medium attracted from painters of the calibre of Pierre Bonnard and Henri de Toulouse-Lautrec. Toulouse-Lautrec had complete mastery of the medium and produced ground-breaking designs with strong images and minimal text, preparing the way for other artists. One of the most successful was the Czech, Alphonse Mucha, who worked mostly in France in his early years. He designed hundreds of posters almost always featuring soft, harmonious colours and seductive young women with long, flowing hair.

Britain was the centre of book illustration, initially inspired by William Blake and then by Walter Crane and other artists associated with the Arts and Crafts movement. The leading illustrator was Aubrey Beardsley, who for many people embodied the decadence and sexuality associated with Art Nouveau. Self-taught, he achieved notoriety through erotic and slightly sinister illustrations for publications such as Oscar Wilde's *Salome* and Sir Thomas Malory's *Morte d'Arthur*. He contributed to various periodicals that helped to disseminate his work. Beardsley died young and his distinctive style, much admired on the Continent, was a great influence on artists such as Gustav Klimt who also painted exotic, sensual femmes fatales.

GLASS

In 1884, an exhibition of glass in Paris showed the work of several glassmakers who had independently experimented with new effects such as cloudy, crackled and aerated glass inspired by the markings on natural stones, quartz and crystals. This work paved the way for some of the greatest artistic and technical achievements of the Art Nouveau movement, particularly by Émile Gallé in France and Louis Comfort Tiffany in the USA.

Émile Gallé, the son of a producer of luxury glassware and ceramics, established a workshop at Nancy in France, two years after being inspired by a display of Japanese glass at the Victoria & Albert Museum in London. Gallé, who had a profound knowledge of botany and zoology, created pieces of decorative glass based on natural shapes such as plants, reptiles and sea creatures. In addition he used a range of special effects such as deeply coloured, multi-layered glass, sometimes carved or etched and decorated with enamels, metallic foils and encrustations of glass. He often decorated his pieces with quotations and lines of verse to help express an emotion he was trying to convey. Gallé inspired a host of imitators including Auguste and Antonin Daum, who had acquired their glassworks in Nancy in lieu of a debt. They hired craftspeople who had trained in Gallé's workshops so the designs are similar but less adventurous, the shapes more conventional and the technique less refined, than Gallé's.

Across the Atlantic, Louis Comfort Tiffany dominated the world of modern glass. He was the son of the owner of the famous jewellers Tiffany in New York. Trained as a painter in Paris, Tiffany first worked as an interior designer and later established his own company, concentrating on glass. Like Gallé, he was a great technical innovator experimenting with blending infinite varieties of colours and inventing new processes such as lustre, iridescence and opalescence. He patented his experiments as Favrile glass.

Tiffany, however, preferred a less abstract interpretation of nature than Gallé and also created glassware, such as lamps which had practical uses.

ABOVE: Dragonfly lampshade made by Tiffany Studios, circa 1900. Tiffany's lampshades were one of the great commercial successes of his company, Tiffany Studios, founded in 1900. The effect of light diffused through coloured glass added to the beauty of the lamps. The lampshades were usually mounted on bronze stands which were also manufactured in Tiffany Studios.

ABOVE: Rhododendron vase by Gallé, circa 1900.

ABOVE: Anemone vasé and Pendant Flower vase made by Daum Frères, circa 1900.

ABOVE: Crocus vase by Gallé, circa 1900, made by combining pieces of coloured glass with the body of the vase when hot, rolling it smooth and carving into it when cool.

CERAMICS

Art Nouveau ceramics made less of an impact than other decorative arts; perhaps because ceramic effects are less showy than glass, or the medium lacked an outstanding ceramist. Studio potters working independently explored iridescent, lustre, crackle, crystalline and metallic glaze effects, or sought to rediscover Oriental glazes. Others experimented with different clays and naturalistic shapes such as vegetables, animals or grotesque masks.

The large commercial pottery manufacturers largely confined their output to painting the usual Art Nouveau images on to pots. Alongside the usual range of ceramics, both studio potters and large manufacturers produced architectural pieces such as chimney surrounds, plaques, friezes and sculptures.

One potter attracted to the early Art Nouveau movement in France was Ernest Chaplet. He rediscovered the formula for making *sang-de-boeuf*, a beautiful deep red Chinese glaze much admired by artists and poets. Chaplet, who had trained at the famous Sèvres factory in France, had great technical expertise and helped the painter Paul Gauguin to make pots which had Art Nouveau characteristics. Another French potter who experimented with clays, glazes and different methods of firing pots was Edmond Lachenal. He invented a process of gilding ceramic surfaces.

In England, the most inventive Art Nouveau pottery was that produced by the four Martin Brothers who worked first in Fulham and then in Southall, Middlesex. They experimented with clays and glazes producing individual pieces of popular salt-glazed stoneware, decorated with grinning birds, fantastic animals and comic masks modelled or incised and carved into the clay. They also produced important architectural pieces for clients.

William Moorcroft, employed as a designer with James McIntyre & Co in Burslem, Staffordshire, perfected a range of ceramics decorated with formal arrangements of typical Art Nouveau motifs such as honeysuckle and peacock feathers outlined in slip (liquid clay).

In Scandanavia and Germany, the large manufacturers such as the Royal Danish Porcelain Factory, Meissen and the Rosenthal Porcelain Company produced some especially elegant and modern pieces, including tableware, which would not look out of place in a modern house today.

OPPOSITE PAGE:
Spanish jardinière
made by Moorcroft,
circa 1912–1916.

ABOVE: Bamboo vase
with a crackle glaze
made by Lachenal,
circa 1893.

RIGHT: A tobacco jar in
the shape of a bird made
by the Martin Brothers.
This pottery is known
as Martinware.

JEWELLERY

D uring the 19th century, Paris was the centre of the fashion industry and its related trades. Jewellers created pieces for royalty, aristocrats and other wealthy individuals using precious metals and gems, especially diamonds, set in traditional styles. Many young designers attracted to the Art Nouveau movement lacked the money to pay for costly jewels. Their use of unconventional and inexpensive materials such as horn, ivory, tortoiseshell, enamels, glass and semi-precious stones, coupled with the emphasis on design, led to some of the most extraordinary and sensual jewellery ever produced.

The greatest exponent of Art Nouveau jewellery was the Frenchman, René Lalique, who trained initially in Paris and then in London. His designs displayed great originality and technical virtuosity using combinations of both precious and non-precious materials considered revolutionary at the time. One of Lalique's clients was the famous French actress, Sarah Bernhardt, whose patronage helped to ensure his reputation as the leading jeweller in Europe.

LEFT: Romeo and Juliet pendant made in gold and enamel by Lalique, circa 1900.

ABOVE: Three pieces of jewellery commissioned by Liberty & Co. The top brooch was designed by Knox. The centre brooch was designed by Charles R. Ashbee, a member of the Arts and Crafts movement. The pendant and chain were designed by King.

Lalique inspired many imitators both in France and elsewhere in Europe and the USA, but no-one else matched his craftsmanship and high level of artistry.

In England, Arthur Liberty commissioned designers such as Archibald Knox and Jessie King to make jewellery that was manufactured in Birmingham for the mass market. Knox was born on the Isle of Man and his designs show the influence of Celtic knots and patterns that are still to be seen on ancient tombstones there. Jessie King was one of the Glasgow School, who mainly created illustrations and books for private presses. Her leaning towards fine, spidery designs was also well suited to jewellery.

ABOVE: A brooch by Lalique, circa 1900. It depicts a sleeping maiden in cast glass overlaid with opalescent enamel. She is set in a silver frame of flowing hair, crowned with four large, open poppies. A baroque pearl hangs from her entwined tresses.

LEFT: Horn hair comb decorated with opals, enamel and gold. Made for the Parisian jewellers Georges Fouquet, circa 1900, in the style of Lalique. Hair combs were in demand for the fashion of upswept hair.

METALWORK

Specially commissioned metal objects for wealthy clients such as decorative boxes, hand mirrors, tea services, vases, bowls, jugs and punch bowls were some of the most extravagantly designed works of art produced during the Art Nouveau period. Other uses for fine metalwork included elaborate bronze, copper and brass mounts for glass and ceramic art pieces, clock cases, lighting fixtures and embellishments for furniture.

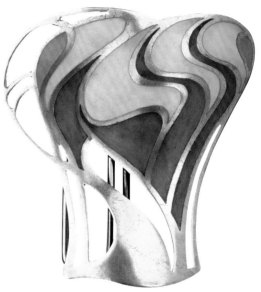

ABOVE: A gilt and enamelled buckle designed by Koloman Moser and made by Georg Scheid, circa 1900.

The Art Nouveau movement not only emphasized fine workmanship, it also honoured craftspeople making their own wares in small studios and workshops. Numerous gold and silversmiths flourished at this time. The most highly regarded worked in Paris, but other European capitals such as London and Berlin, and also New York, attracted accomplished gold and silversmiths. Many were better known as jewellers, as was René Lalique, who made a variety of small luxury objects including scent bottles, silver mounts for glass cups and vases, and walking-stick handles.

Much Art Nouveau silver was decorated with enamels, mother-of-pearl or semi-

ABOVE: An ice bucket by Carlo Bugatti. Like Gaudí in Spain, Bugatti was an isolated star in Italy, who drew on Spanish-Moorish influences.

precious jewels, since too much shiny silver was considered unattractive. Enamelling was especially popular: the craft did not demand special skills and the small kilns required to fuse the enamel on to metal did not take up much room in the workshop.

In Britain, silversmithing was one of the few crafts to embrace Art Nouveau to any great extent. Liberty & Co dominated the production of metalwork, silver being marketed under the trade name of 'Cymric' and pewter as 'Tudric'. The goods, manufactured using production techniques, were often given a hammered finish to give a handcrafted appearance. Both ranges, from standard items such as muffin dishes and christening sets to costly sporting trophies and punch bowls, were a huge commercial success.

BELOW: A tea and coffee service, circa *1900, anon.*

ABOVE: A silver mantel clock decorated with enamel from Liberty's Cymric range, 1903.

SCULPTURE

On the Continent, particularly in France, there was a gradual demand throughout the 19th century for small scale sculpture for the home. Art Nouveau sculptors responded to the idea of an integrated artistic environment and also to the idea that all household objects, whatever their function, should be aesthetically pleasing. In addition to producing small statuettes they also made sculptural chimney-piece surrounds, centrepieces and light fixtures.

The traditional mythological, allegorical and historical subject matter was largely abandoned. Sculptors drew on the same range of themes as other arts, but none was so popular as the theme of 'woman'. Dreamy young maidens, languorous nymphs and sultry temptresses were portrayed in every conceivable way, from the grandiose to the sentimental. One of the most popular models was the American entertainer Loïe Fuller, who in 1892 arrived in Paris and established herself at the Folies-Bergère. She danced beneath flickering rainbows of constantly changing electric lights, manipulating her flowing dresses with

wands attached to the hem. Loïe took Paris by storm and she was a source of inspiration to many writers, artists and designers.

Raoul Larche was one such sculptor who succumbed to the charms of Loïe. He made sculptural lamps based on her performances. Another French sculptor, Louis Chalon, trained originally as a painter, then became an illustrator, jeweller and even a designer of royal capes. He specialized in mixtures of women and insect or women-flowers disporting themselves on vases, centrepieces for tables and other items.

In Austria, Gustav Gurschner followed the trend for smaller sculpture. Originally a sculptor working on monumental sculpture and portrait busts, he turned his hand to household objects such as door-knockers, candlesticks, mirrors and lamps, many of which were modelled on young women and cast in bronze.

RIGHT: Gurschner produced cast bronze lamps incorporating seashells that housed electric light bulbs. The natural luminosity of the shell, lit from within, produced a very pleasing light.

ABOVE: This bust called Sylvia *was made by Emmanuel Villanis, who specialized in portrait busts.*

RIGHT: This lamp sculpture of Loïe Fuller is by Larche, one of the most notable sculptors of the Art Nouveau movement.

19

THE LEGACY of ART NOUVEAU

Art Nouveau was a relatively short-lived movement that had declined by the outbreak of the First World War. As it had become more popular, it was commercially exploited and diminished in quality and taste. The best artists lost interest because they produced work that was expensive and unsuitable for mass production. Second-rate artists began to put meaningless lines on traditional objects that had not been designed specially.

The movement had never been popular or widespread and most British artists condemned it as being decadent and bizarre. Walter Crane described Art Nouveau as a 'strange, decorative disease'. Charles Voysey, the architect, said that the style 'was out of harmony with our national character and climate'. Two of the greatest British talents, Aubrey Beardsley and Charles Rennie Mackintosh, both very influential on the Continent, were widely condemned by their countryfolk.

Nevertheless, Art Nouveau succeeded in clearing away the outworn ideas of the 19th century to make way for the development of modern art in the 20th century. Henri van de Velde founded a school that later became the Bauhaus, the most famous school of architecture, art and design of modern times. Peter Behrens, professor of architecture in Munich, and once an Art Nouveau designer himself, taught Walter Gropius, Ludwig Mies van der Rohe and Le Corbusier. They were later to become three of the greatest names in architecture of the 20th century. Today, the work of many of the greatest practitioners of Art Nouveau commands huge sums of money and is eagerly sought by collectors all over the world.

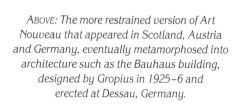

ABOVE CENTRE: The more flamboyant version of Art Nouveau that flourished in Belgium and France was superseded by Art Deco which grew out of a conscious effort to make design more responsive to the new machine-age. Victoire, an Art Deco glass mascot, was designed by Lalique after 1928.

ABOVE: The more restrained version of Art Nouveau that appeared in Scotland, Austria and Germany, eventually metamorphosed into architecture such as the Bauhaus building, designed by Gropius in 1925–6 and erected at Dessau, Germany.